Little People, BIG DREAMS®

DAVID ATTENBOROUGH

Written by
Maria Isabel Sánchez Vegara

Illustrated by
Mikyo Noh

Frances Lincoln
Children's Books

Little David grew up in Leicester, England, with his parents and two brothers. His father was the head of the local university and they lived on campus: a great place for curious minds.

David loved nature and animals. Ants, birds,
chameleons… he was fascinated by all the species he read
about in books and wished he could meet them in real life.

He often went for long cycling trips to find and collect fossils. There was something amazing about plants and animals that were thousands of years old.

One day, David received a parcel from
a friend with a new piece for his collection –
a dried seahorse! It wasn't his birthday, but
it was the day he decided to become a naturalist.

David studied geology and zoology and obtained a degree in natural science. But he didn't want to just observe animals — he wanted to meet them, too.

David started to work as a broadcaster in television, a new technology at the time. He brought animals from the zoo to the studio. They were very entertaining guests!

But David wanted to film the animals in their natural
habitats – their homes. He started to go on trips all over
the world. Wherever he went, he made new friends.

He met turtles on the Galápagos Islands and gorillas in the African jungle. When he visited Antarctica, he was introduced to all the members of a penguin family.

One of his programmes, 'Wildlife on One', became the most popular in British history. It was a brilliant show about biology that united audiences of all generations.

Later, David was honoured for his incredible documentaries about life on our planet. He also received a knighthood and is today called 'Sir David'.

Electrotettix
Attenboroughi

Cascolus Ravitis

RRS SIR DAVID ATTENBOROUGH

Euptych
Attenboro

Materpiscis
Attenborough

Microleo
Attenboroughi

Prethopalpus
Attenboroughi

Nepenthes
Attenboroughii

Many animals and plants were named after him:
a rare butterfly, a snail, a prehistoric lion, a spider...
even a carnivorous plant!

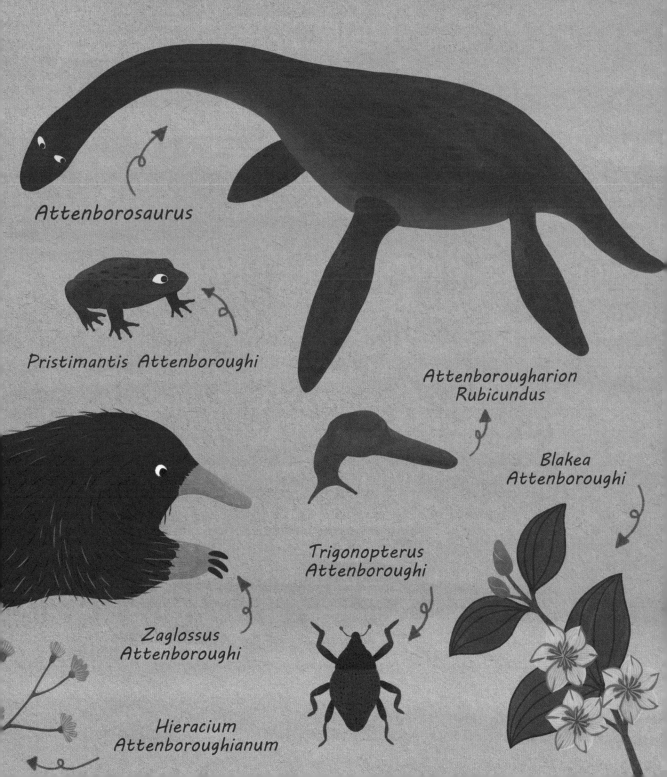

Attenborosaurus

Pristimantis Attenboroughi

Attenborougharion
Rubicundus

Blakea
Attenboroughi

Trigonopterus
Attenboroughi

Zaglossus
Attenboroughi

Hieracium
Attenboroughianum

Still today, David cares about the natural world. Wherever he goes, he encourages people to do their best to look after it, and believes that humans have the power to preserve it.

And little David still looks at the world as if it's huge and unexplored. Because there are always new things to discover if you take the time to look for them.

DAVID ATTENBOROUGH

(Born 1926)

c. 1936

1955

David Attenborough was born into an educational family in Leicester, England. His mother was a linguist and his father, a professor. As a child, fossil hunting and collecting nature specimens became David's passion. This appetite for learning stayed with him, and as a young man David won a scholarship to study zoology and geology at Cambridge University. His studies were paused when he was called up for national service in the Royal Navy in 1947, but he later returned to study another degree in anthropology. Combining a love for the natural world with an understanding of human behaviour, David became known for his unique approach to broadcasting at the BBC. Speaking in a hushed tone full of excitement, David filmed

1956

2015

his first programme in 1957: 'Zoo Quest'. He wanted to find ways to connect audiences to the natural world, and the opportunity to do so came about when colour television was introduced to the BBC in 1967. His groundbreaking series 'Life on Earth' transported audiences from their living rooms to the wild in a totally new way. This was the first of many pioneering shows, including 'Wildlife on One', 'The Private Life of Plants' and 'Blue Planet', all of which changed human understanding about our place in nature. David believed that "no one will protect what they don't care about; and no one will care about what they have never experienced." In his nineties, David continues to make audiences all over the world care.

Want to find out more about **David Attenborough?**
Have a read of these great books:

Super Scientists: David Attenborough by Sarah Ridley
David Attenborough: Naturalist Visionary by Sonya Newland

Brimming with creative inspiration, how-to projects, and useful information to enrich your everyday life, quarto.com is a favorite destination for those pursuing their interests and passions.

Text copyright © 2020 Maria Isabel Sánchez Vegara. Illustrations copyright © 2020 Mikyo Noh.
Original concept of the series by Maria Isabel Sánchez Vegara, published by Alba Editorial, S.L.U.
Little People Big Dreams and Pequeña & Grande are registered trademarks of Alba Editorial, S.L.U. for books, publications and e-books. Produced under licence from Alba Editorial, S.L.U.

First published in the UK in 2020 by Frances Lincoln Children's Books, an imprint of The Quarto Group.
The Old Brewery, 6 Blundell Street, London N7 9BH, United Kingdom.
T (0)20 7700 6700 **www.quarto.com**
First published in Spain in 2020 under the title Pequeño & Grande David Attenborough
by Alba Editorial, S.L.U., Baixada de Sant Miquel, 1, 08002 Barcelona www.albaeditorial.es
All rights reserved.

A catalogue record for this book is available from the British Library.
ISBN 978-0-7112-4563-1
Set in Futura BT.

Published by Katie Cotton • Designed by Karissa Santos
Edited by Rachel Williams and Katy Flint • Production by Nicolas Zeifman

Manufactured in Guangdong, China CC122021

14

Photographic acknowledgements (pages 28-29, from left to right) 1. David Attenborough school photograph, c. 1936 © Leicester Mercury Picture 2. David Attenborough with his son, Robert, and coatimundi © 1955 PA/PA Archive/PA Images 3. A portrait of British naturalist and broadcaster David Attenborough, 1956 © Popperfoto via Getty Images 4. David Attenborough, 2015 © Neale Haynes via Getty Images

Collect the Little People, BIG DREAMS® series:

FRIDA KAHLO	**COCO CHANEL** 	**MAYA ANGELOU**	**AMELIA EARHART** 	**AGATHA CHRISTIE** 	**MARIE CURIE** 	**ROSA PARKS** 	**AUDREY HEPBURN** 
EMMELINE PANKHURST 	**ELLA FITZGERALD** 	**ADA LOVELACE** 	**JANE AUSTEN** 	**GEORGIA O'KEEFFE** 	**HARRIET TUBMAN** 	**ANNE FRANK** 	**MOTHER TERESA** 
JOSEPHINE BAKER 	**L. M. MONTGOMERY** 	**JANE GOODALL** 	**SIMONE DE BEAUVOIR** 	**MUHAMMAD ALI** 	**STEPHEN HAWKING** 	**MARIA MONTESSORI** 	**VIVIENNE WESTWOOD**
MAHATMA GANDHI 	**DAVID BOWIE** 	**WILMA RUDOLPH** 	**DOLLY PARTON** 	**BRUCE LEE** 	**RUDOLF NUREYEV** 	**ZAHA HADID** 	**MARY SHELLEY** 
MARTIN LUTHER KING JR. 	**DAVID ATTENBOROUGH** 	**ASTRID LINDGREN** 	**EVONNE GOOLAGONG** 	**BOB DYLAN** 	**ALAN TURING** 	**BILLIE JEAN KING** 	**GRETA THUNBERG** 
JESSE OWENS 	**JEAN-MICHEL BASQUIAT** 	**ARETHA FRANKLIN** 	**CORAZON AQUINO** 	**PELÉ** 	**ERNEST SHACKLETON** 	**STEVE JOBS** 	**AYRTON SENNA** 
LOUISE BOURGEOIS 	**ELTON JOHN** 	**JOHN LENNON** 	**PRINCE** 	**CHARLES DARWIN** 	**CAPTAIN TOM MOORE** 	**HANS CHRISTIAN ANDERSEN**	**STEVIE WONDER** 

MEGAN RAPINOE

MARY ANNING

MALALA YOUSAFZAI

ANDY WARHOL

RUPAUL

MICHELLE OBAMA

MINDY KALING

IRIS APFEL

ROSALIND FRANKLIN

RUTH BADER GINSBURG

MARILYN MONROE

KAMALA HARRIS

ALBERT EINSTEIN

CHARLES DICKENS

YOKO ONO

MICHAEL JORDAN

NELSON MANDELA

PABLO PICASSO

AMANDA GORMAN

GLORIA STEINEM

FLORENCE NIGHTINGALE

HARRY HOUDINI

J.R.R. TOLKIEN

ACTIVITY BOOKS

STICKER ACTIVITY BOOK

COLOURING BOOK

LITTLE ME, BIG DREAMS JOURNAL

Discover more about the series at www.littlepeoplebigdreams.com

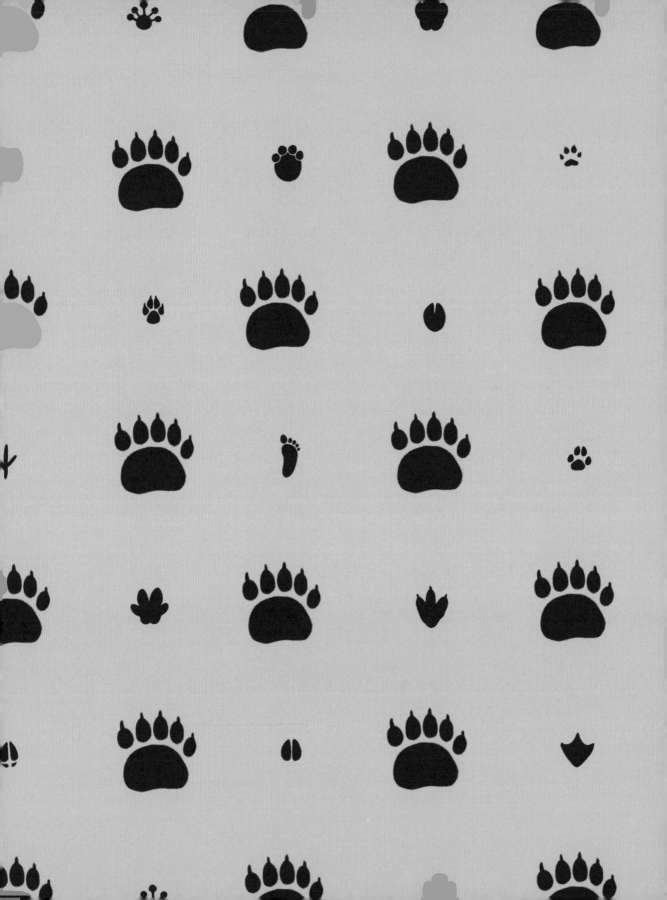